EXTREME PRESIDENTIAL TRIVIA

Little Known Facts About Our Presidents

Bradley W. Rasch

iUniverse, Inc.
Bloomington

Extreme Presidential Trivia
Little Known Facts About Our Presidents

iUniverse books may be ordered through booksellers or by contacting:

*iUniverse
1663 Liberty Drive
Bloomington, IN 47403
www.iuniverse.com
1-800-Authors (1-800-288-4677)*

*ISBN: 978-1-4759-3303-1 (sc)
ISBN: 978-1-4759-3304-8 (hc)
ISBN: 978-1-4759-3305-5 (e)*

Library of Congress Control Number: 2012910525

Printed in the United States of America

iUniverse rev. date: 6/7/2012

Introduction

After writing a previous book, *Explaining and Defending American Government,* the author was encouraged to write about our presidents and address facts about them that few of us know.

Many men have served (and hopefully soon, women). We will start with some lists, then fairly well-known trivia, and finally we will venture into the obscure and little known.

OTHER BOOKS BY BRADLEY W. RASCH

Psychology: The Stuff You Can Really Use

Extreme Trivia: The Chicago Professional Sports Trivia They Do Not Want You to Know

Explaining and Defending American Government

PRESIDENTS

Presidents
1. George Washington
2. John Adams
3. Thomas Jefferson
4. James Madison
5. James Monroe
6. John Quincy Adams
7. Andrew Jackson
8. Martin Van Buren
9. William Henry Harrison
10. John Tyler
11. James K. Polk
12. Zachary Taylor
13. Millard Fillmore
14. Franklin Pierce
15. James Buchanan
16. Abraham Lincoln
17. Andrew Johnson
18. Ulysses S. Grant
19. Rutherford B. Hayes
20. James Garfield
21. Chester A. Arthur
22. Grover Cleveland

23. Benjamin Harrison
24. Grover Cleveland
25. William McKinley
26. Theodore Roosevelt
27. William Howard Taft
28. Woodrow Wilson
29. Warren G. Harding
30. Calvin Coolidge
31. Herbert Hoover
32. Franklin D. Roosevelt
33. Harry S. Truman
34. Dwight D. Eisenhower
35. John F. Kennedy
36. Lyndon B. Johnson
37. Richard M. Nixon
38. Gerald R. Ford
39. James Carter
40. Ronald Reagan
41. George H. W. Bush
42. William J. Clinton
43. George W. Bush
44. Barack Obama

PART ONE

THE LISTS

OUR PRESIDENTS AND VICE PRESIDENTS

President	Vice President
George Washington (1789–1797)	John Adams (1789–1797)
John Adams (1797–1801)	Thomas Jefferson (1797–1801)
Thomas Jefferson (1801–1809)	Aaron Burr (1801–1805)
	George Clinton (1805–1809)
James Madison (1809–1817)	George Clinton (1809–1812)
	none (1812–1813)
	Elbridge Gerry (1813–1814)
	none (1814–1817)
James Monroe (1817–1825)	Daniel D. Tompkins (1817–1825)
John Quincy Adams (1825–1829)	John C. Calhoun (1825–1829)
Andrew Jackson (1829–1837)	John C. Calhoun (1829–1832)
	none (1832–1833)
	Martin Van Buren (1833–1837)
Martin Van Buren (1837–1841)	Richard M. Johnson (1837–1841)

William Henry Harrison (1841)	John Tyler (1841)
John Tyler (1841–1845)	none (1841–1845)
James K. Polk (1845–1849)	George M. Dallas (1845–1849)
Zachary Taylor (1849–1850)	Millard Fillmore (1849–1850)
Millard Fillmore (1850–1853)	none (1850–1853)
Franklin Pierce (1853–1857)	William King (1853)
	none (1853–1857)
James Buchanan (1857–1861)	John C. Breckinridge (1857–1861)
Abraham Lincoln (1861–1865)	Hannibal Hamlin (1861–1865)
	Andrew Johnson (1865)
Andrew Johnson (1865–1869)	none (1865–1869)
Ulysses S. Grant (1869–1877)	Schuyler Colfax (1869–1873)
	Henry Wilson (1873–1875)
	none (1875–1877)
Rutherford B. Hayes (1877–1881)	William Wheeler (1877–1881)
James A. Garfield (1881)	Chester Arthur (1881)
Chester Arthur (1881–1885)	none (1881–1885)
Grover Cleveland (1885–1889)	Thomas Hendricks (1885)
	none (1885–1889)
Benjamin Harrison (1889–1893)	Levi P. Morton (1889–1893)
Grover Cleveland (1893–1897)	Adlai E. Stevenson (1893–1897)
William McKinley (1897–1901)	Garret Hobart (1897–1899)
	none (1899–1901)
	Theodore Roosevelt (1901)
Theodore Roosevelt (1901–1909)	none (1901–1905)

	Charles Fairbanks (1905–1909)
William Howard Taft (1909–1913)	James S. Sherman (1909–1912)
	none (1912–1913)
Woodrow Wilson (1913–1921)	Thomas R. Marshall (1913–1921)
Warren G. Harding (1921–1923)	Calvin Coolidge (1921–1923)
Calvin Coolidge (1923–1929)	none (1923–1925)
	Charles Dawes (1925–1929)
Herbert Hoover (1929–1933)	Charles Curtis (1929–1933)
Franklin D. Roosevelt (1933–1945)	John Nance Garner (1933–1941)
	Henry A. Wallace (1941–1945)
	Harry S. Truman (1945)
Harry S. Truman (1945–1953)	none (1945–1949)
	Alben Barkley (1949–1953)
Dwight D. Eisenhower (1953–1961)	Richard Nixon (1953–1961)
John F. Kennedy (1961–1963)	Lyndon B. Johnson (1961–1963)
Lyndon B. Johnson (1963–1969)	none (1963–1965)
	Hubert Humphrey (1965–1969)
Richard Nixon (1969–1974)	Spiro Agnew (1969–1973)
	none (1973)
	Gerald Ford (1973–1974)
Gerald Ford (1974–1977)	none (1974)
	Nelson Rockefeller (1974–1977)
Jimmy Carter (1977–1981)	Walter Mondale (1977–1981)
Ronald Reagan (1981–1989)	George Bush (1981–1989)
George Bush (1989–1993)	Dan Quayle (1989–1993)

Bill Clinton (1993–2001)   Al Gore (1993–2001)
George W. Bush (2001–2009)   Dick Cheney (2001–2009)
Barack Obama (2009–present)   Joe Biden (2009–present)

PRESIDENTS WHO DIED IN OFFICE

1. **William Henry Harrison:** Our ninth president died in 1841 of pneumonia and pleurisy.
2. **Zachary Taylor:** The twelfth president died in 1850 of bilious fever, typhoid fever, and cholera morbus following a heat stroke.
3. **Abraham Lincoln:** The sixteenth president was assassinated in 1865. Lincoln was the first of four presidents to be assassinated.
4. **James Garfield:** The twentieth president was assassinated in 1881.
5. **William McKinley:** The twenty-fifth president was assassinated in 1901.
6. **Warren G. Harding:** The twenty-ninth president died in1923 of a suspected heart attack.
7. **Franklin Delano Roosevelt:** The thirty-second president died in 1945 of a cerebral hemorrhage
8. **John F. Kennedy:** The thirty-fifth president was assassinated in 1963.

PRESIDENTS BORN BEFORE THE UNITED STATES BECAME A COUNTRY

1. George Washington
2. John Adams
3. Thomas Jefferson
4. James Madison
5. James Monroe
6. John Quincy Adams
7. Andrew Jackson
8. William Henry Harrison

PRESIDENTS WHO WERE ATTORNEYS

1. John Adams
2. Thomas Jefferson
3. John Quincy Adams
4. Andrew Jackson
5. Martin Van Buren
6. John Tyler
7. James Polk
8. Millard Fillmore
9. Franklin Pierce
10. James Buchanan
11. Rutherford Hayes
12. Chester Arthur
13. Grover Cleveland
14. Benjamin Harrison
15. William McKinley
16. William Taft
17. Woodrow Wilson
18. Calvin Coolidge
19. Franklin Roosevelt
20. Richard Nixon
21. Gerald Ford
22. Bill Clinton

PRESIDENTS WHO FIRST
SERVED AS VICE PRESIDENTS

1. John Adams, under George Washington
2. Thomas Jefferson, under John Adams
3. Martin Van Buren, under Andrew Jackson
4. John Tyler, under William Henry Harrison
5. Millard Fillmore, under Zachary Taylor
6. Andrew Johnson, under Abraham Lincoln
7. Chester Arthur, under James Garfield
8. Theodore Roosevelt, under William McKinley
9. Calvin Coolidge, under Warren Harding
10. Harry Truman, under Franklin Roosevelt
11. Lyndon Johnson, under John Kennedy
12. Richard Nixon, under Dwight Eisenhower
13. Gerald Ford, under Richard Nixon
14. George Bush, under Ronald Reagan

PRESIDENTS WHO LOST THE POPULAR VOTE BUT BECAME PRESIDENT BY HAVING MORE VOTES FROM THE ELECTORAL COLLEGE

1. Rutherford Hayes—Samuel Tilden won the popular vote.
2. Benjamin Harrison—Sitting president Grover Cleveland won the popular vote.
3. George W. Bush—Al Gore took the popular vote, and the Supreme Court ended up deciding this election.

CHIEF EXECUTIVES WHO WERE THOUGHT TO HAVE HAD PROBLEMS WITH ALCOHOL

1. Franklin Pierce
2. Ulysses Grant
3. George W. Bush

PRESIDENTS KNOWN TO HAVE CHILDREN OUTSIDE OF MARRIAGE

1. Thomas Jefferson (with one of his slaves)
2. Grover Cleveland
3. Warren Harding

PRESIDENTS WHO WERE ALLEGED TO HAVE HAD AFFAIRS

1. Thomas Jefferson
2. James Garfield
3. Warren Harding
4. Franklin Roosevelt
5. John Kennedy
6. Lyndon Johnson
7. Bill Clinton

PRESIDENTS WHO WERE SLAVE OWNERS

1. George Washington
2. Thomas Jefferson
3. James Madison
4. Andrew Jackson
5. James Polk
6. Zachary Taylor

PRESIDENTS WHO DID NOT HAVE CHILDREN

1. James Madison
2. James Polk
3. James Buchanan

PRESIDENTS WITH ADOPTED CHILDREN

1. George Washington
2. Andrew Jackson
3. Ronald Reagan

PRESIDENTS WHO DID PLAY-BY-PLAY OF CHICAGO CUBS GAMES ON THE RADIO

1. Ronald Reagan (For obvious reasons, he did not often speak of this.)

PRESIDENTS WHO WERE FREEMASONS

1. George Washington
2. James Monroe
3. Andrew Jackson
4. James Polk
5. James Buchanan
6. Andrew Johnson
7. James Garfield
8. William McKinley
9. Theodore Roosevelt
10. Howard Taft
11. Warren Harding
12. Franklin Roosevelt
13. Harry Truman
14. Gerald Ford

PRESIDENTS WHO
WERE BOY SCOUTS

1. John F. Kennedy
2. Gerald Ford
3. Bill Clinton
4. George W. Bush
5. Barack Obama (the Indonesian equivalent)

PRESIDENTS WHO
WENT TO HARVARD

1. Barack Obama
2. George W. Bush
3. John Adams
4. John Quincy Adams
5. Rutherford B. Hayes,
6. Theodore Roosevelt
7. Franklin D. Roosevelt
8. John F. Kennedy

LIST OF FIRST LADIES

President	First Lady
George Washington	Martha Dandridge
John Adams	Abigail Smith
Thomas Jefferson	Martha Wayles Skelton
James Madison	Dolly Payne Todd
James Monroe	Elizabeth "Eliza" Kortright
John Quincy Adams	Louisa Catherine Johnson
Andrew Jackson	Rachel Donelson Robards
Martin Van Buren	Hannah Hoes
William Henry Harrison	Anna Tuthill Symmes
John Tyler	Julia Gardiner
James Knox Polk	Sarah Childress
Zachary Taylor	Margaret Mackall Smith
Millard Fillmore	Abigail Powers
Franklin Pierce	Jane Means Appleton
James Buchanan	-
Abraham Lincoln	Mary Todd
Andrew Johnson	Eliza McCardle
Ulysses Simpson Grant	Julia Boggs Dent

Rutherford Birchard Hayes	Lucy Ware Webb
James Abram Garfield	Lucretia Rudolph
Chester Alan Arthur	Ellen Lewis Herndon
Grover Cleveland	Frances Fulsom
Benjamin Harrison	Caroline Lavinia Scott
Grover Cleveland	Frances Fulsom
William McKinley	Ida Saxton
Theodore Roosevelt	Edith Kermit Carow
William Howard Taft	Helen Herron
Woodrow Wilson	Edith Bolling Galt
Warren Gamaliel Harding	Florence Kling DeWolf
Calvin Coolidge	Anna Grace Goodhew
Herbert Clark Hoover	Lou Henry
Franklin Delano Roosevelt	Anna Eleanor Roosevelt
Harry S. Truman	Elizabeth "Bess" Virginia Wallace
Dwight David Eisenhower	Mary "Mamie" Geneva Doud
John Fitzgerald Kennedy	Jacqueline Lee Bouvier
Lyndon Baines Johnson	Claudia "Lady Bird" Alta Taylor
Richard Milhous Nixon	Thelma Patricia "Pat" Catherine Ryan
Gerald Rudolph Ford	Elizabeth "Betty" Bloomer Warren
James Earl Carter	Eleanor Rosalynn Smith
Ronald Wilson Reagan	Nancy Davis
George Herbert Walker Bush	Barbara Pierce
William Jefferson Clinton	Hillary Rodham
George Walker Bush	Laura Welch
Barack Obama	Michelle Robinson

PRESIDENTS WHO HAVE WON THE NOBEL PEACE PRIZE

1. Theodore Roosevelt (1905)
2. Woodrow Wilson (1919)
3. Jimmy Carter Jr. (2002)
4. Barack Obama (2009)

PRESIDENTS WHO WERE PEANUT FARMERS AND NUCLEAR SUBMARINE COMMANDERS BEFORE TAKING OFFICE

1. Jimmy Carter

OUR PRESIDENTS ARE
NOT A DULL LOT

JIMMY CARTER CLAIMED THAT he saw a UFO. Most know he was a peanut farmer, but we often forget he also was a nuclear submarine commander.

CALVIN COOLIDGE WAS COMMONLY known for being a man of few words; what many do not know is that he enjoyed having his head rubbed with petroleum jelly while he ate breakfast in bed.

GERALD FORD WAS ADOPTED; his name before he was adopted was Leslie Lynch King. He was never elected vice president; rather, he was appointed by Nixon to replace Spiro Agnew, who resigned in disgrace. Ford also was never elected president. He succeeded Nixon, who also resigned in disgrace.

JAMES GARFIELD COULD SIMULTANEOUSLY write in Latin with one hand while writing in Greek with his other hand. George W. Bush reportedly could write in English with one hand, though some people dispute this.

WARREN G. HARDING MAY have been a gambling addict; he lost the White House china in a game of poker.

ANDREW JACKSON WAS INVOLVED in over a hundred duels. Before being president he was a tailor, and he only wore suits that he had made himself (like Gandhi in some ways, very much not like the Mahatma in others).

IN PRE-VIAGRA DAYS, JOHN Tyler had fifteen kids (eight with one wife, seven with another). His last child was born when he was seventy (and we think Bill Clinton was a hound dog).

JAMES MADISON NEVER WEIGHED over a hundred pounds, and William Howard Taft was so fat he once became stuck in the White House bathtub.

GEORGE BUSH THE ELDER was responsible for a new word in the Japanese language. The word means to vomit publicly—something Bush famously did once while visiting Japan. He threw up on the Japanese prime minister during a banquet.

JOHN QUINCY ADAMS USED to skinny dip in the Potomac River.

THOMAS JEFFERSON HAD CHILDREN with his slave, who was a half-sister of his dead wife.

HONEST ABE LINCOLN WAS a licensed bartender and was the only US president to own a patent.

BARRACK OBAMA COLLECTS *SPIDER-MAN* and *Conan the Barbarian* comic books.

THIRD PARTY CANDIDATES

Candidate	Party or Parties	Year(s)
William Wirt	Anti-Masonic	1832
James G. Birney	Liberty	1840, 1844
Martin Van Buren	Free Soil	1848
John Hale	Free Soil	1852
Millard Fillmore	American (Know-Nothing)	1856
John C. Breckinridge	Southern Democratic	1860
John Bell	Constitutional Union	1860
Victoria Woodhull	Equal Rights	1872
James B. Weaver	Greenback, Populist (People's)	1880, 1892
Benjamin Butler	Greenback	1884
Clinton B. Fisk	Prohibition	1888
Alson J. Streeter	Union Labor	1888
John Bidwell	Prohibition	1892
Eugene V. Debs	Socialist	1900, 1904, 1908, 1912, 1920

John Woolley	Prohibition	1900
Silas Swallow	Prohibition	1904
Thomas Watson	Populist	1904, 1908
Eugene Chafin	Prohibition	1908, 1912
Arthur Reimer	Socialist Labor	1912, 1916
Theodore Roosevelt	Progressive (Bull Moose)	1912
Allan L. Benson	Socialist	1916
J. Frank Hanly	Prohibition	1916
William Z. Foster	Communist	1924, 1928, 1932
Robert LaFollette	Progressive, Socialist	1924
Norman Thomas	Socialist	1928, 1932, 1936, 1940, 1944, 1948
Verne Reynolds	Socialist Labor	1928, 1932
John Aiken	Socialist Labor	1936, 1940
Earl Browder	Communist	1936, 1940
William Lemke	Union	1936
Claude Watson	Prohibition	1944, 1948
Edward Teichert	Socialist Labor	1944, 1948
Farrell Dobbs	Socialist Workers	1948, 1952, 1956, 1960
Henry A. Wallace	Progressive	1948
Strom Thurmond	States Rights	1948
Eric Hass	Socialist Labor	1952, 1956, 1960, 1964
Henry Krajewski	Poor Man's, American Third	1952, 1956
Darlington Hoopes	Socialist	1952, 1956
Douglas MacArthur	Constitution, America First	1952
E. Harold Munn	Prohibition	1964, 1968, 1972

Eugene McCarthy	Independent, Consumers	1968, 1976, 1988
George Wallace	American Independent	1968
Dick Gregory	Freedom and Peace	1968
Eldridge Cleaver	Peace and Freedom	1968
Gus Hall	Communist	1972, 1976, 1980, 1984
John Schmitz	American Independent	1972
Benjamin Spock	People's	1972
John Hospers	Libertarian	1972
Lyndon LaRouche	US Labor, National Economic Recovery, Independent	1976, 1984, 1988, 1992
Ben Bubar	Prohibition	1976, 1980
Lester Maddox	American Independent	1976
John Anderson	Independent	1980
Ed Clark	Libertarian	1980
David McReynolds	Socialist	1980, 2000
Earl Dodge	Prohibition	1984, 1988, 1992, 1996, 2000, 2004
Delmar Dennis	American	1984, 1988
Ed Winn	Workers League	1984, 1988
Larry Holmes	Workers World	1984, 1988
Ron Paul	Libertarian (1988), Various and Write-In (2008)	1988, 2008
Lenora Fulani	New Alliance	1988, 1992
James Warren	Socialist Workers	1988, 1992
Jack Herer	Grassroots	1988, 1992
John Hagelin	Natural Law	1992, 1996, 2000

Howard Phillips	US Taxpayers, Constitution	1992, 1996, 2000
Andre Marrou	Libertarian	1992
Ross Perot	Independent, Reform	1992, 1996
Isabell Masters	Looking Back	1992, 1996
Ralph Nader	Green, Reform, Independent	1996, 2000, 2004, 2008
Harry Browne	Libertarian	1996, 2000
James Harris	Socialist Workers	1996, 2000, 2004, 2008
Monica Moorehead	Workers World	1996, 2000
Pat Buchanan	Reform	2000
Michael Badnarik	Libertarian	2004
Bob Barr	Libertarian	2008
Chuck Baldwin	Constitution	2008
Cynthia McKinney	Green	2008

PART TWO

THE PRESIDENTS

GEORGE WASHINGTON

HE GREW MARIJUANA ON the family farm. (It was legal at the time.)

He was the only president to free his slaves.

He was the only chief executive to be elected unanimously.

He had false teeth, none of which were made of wood. They were made from elephant, cow, walrus, and other animals. Some were even made from other humans' teeth.

He had his horses' teeth brushed every day.

He did not believe in bathing, thinking it unhealthy.

Did Martha ever actually kiss this guy?

JOHN ADAMS

JOHN ADAMS, OUR SECOND chief executive, was called "His Rotundity" because he was short in stature and rather heavyset. He had a dog named Satan (certainly that would make him unelectable today). His great-great-grandparents were Pilgrims who landed on Plymouth Rock. When he and the first lady set out to the White House for the first time to reside there, they got lost. If cable news shows had existed at the time, they would have had a field day with the Adams family.

THOMAS JEFFERSON

OUR THIRD LEADER WAS fluent in six languages (six more than our forty-third president). He was the inventor of the swivel chair and popularized tomatoes (before he advocated eating them, many thought they were poisonous). He was also the inventor of the pedometer. Perhaps he was too smart to be electable today.

JAMES MADISON

Number four was our tiniest chief, weighing in at less than one hundred pounds. (He was the Michael Bloomberg of his time.) The man known as "The Father of the Constitution" may have made a more valuable contribution: we may never have enjoyed casual Fridays without him. He was the first president to wear pants instead of knee britches.

JAMES MONROE

Monroe, our fifth president, had a city named after him: Monrovia, Liberia. Liberia was created by American abolitionists for slaves so that they could be freed and return to Africa.

James Monroe preferred to be called Colonel, instead of President, because he was very proud of his Revolutionary War service.

Monroe was a direct descendent of King Edward II of England.

Monroe did not author the doctrine that bears his name. His secretary of state did.

JOHN QUINCY ADAMS

President Adams enjoyed swimming naked in the Potomac. He was serious about exercise and was lucky to have lived in a time when there were no photojournalists. His wife raised silkworms in the White House. His relatives waited until 1951 to release his diaries, which were quite extensive. They shed no light on his swimming habits.

ANDREW JACKSON

HE LEFT HIS OWN inauguration party because it was getting way out of hand. There were too many people in attendance, so he spent the night in a hotel.

He was the first president to ride in a train.

Jackson never set foot out of the United States.

He was a military man and an Indian fighter. Ironically, he adopted a Creek Indian, Lyncota, as his son.

He was responsible for bringing running water to the White House.

MARTIN VAN BUREN

He was our first president born an American citizen.

He created the term *okay*, which is now used around the world.

He owned two pet tiger cubs. He obviously served before the existence of PETA.

He was bilingual—he spoke Dutch.

Though he was a lawyer, he never attended college (which was not uncommon at the time).

WILLIAM HENRY HARRISON

OUR NINTH PRESIDENT SERVED only one month. He died from pneumonia after giving a two-hour inaugural address in the cold without wearing a jacket. (Sounds like he may have fit in well with the 2012 GOP field.)

Old Tippecanoe was our first president to receive over one million votes.

In this pre-PETA era, he owned a pet cow and a pet goat.

He owned a distillery and produced whiskey.

JOHN TYLER

HE WAS THE FIRST vice president to take office due to the death of the sitting president. This hurt his legitimacy, and he was often referred to as "the accidental president."

He was on his knees playing marbles when he was told he had become president. (This alone should qualify him for Mount Rushmore.)

He was the first president who lost a wife while serving.

He joined the Confederacy after serving as president. He was elected to the Confederate House of Representatives but died before serving.

Viewed as a traitor, he was stripped of his US citizenship.

Jimmy Carter had Tyler's citizenship restored.

Tyler's second wife was responsible for having "Hail to the Chief" played when a president is introduced.

A city in Texas was named after him.

A busy man, he had fifteen children.

He never had a vice president.

JAMES K. POLK

OUR ELEVENTH PRESIDENT SERVED one term, from 1845 to 1849.

A brave young man, at the age of seventeen, he had an operation for gallstones. While this may seem unremarkable, it must be pointed out that anesthesia had not yet been invented.

Polk was the first president to be in power coast to coast.

Polk was a workaholic before the term existed. He did not believe in leisure time. Indeed, he was quoted as saying, "No president who performs his duties faithfully and conscientiously can have any leisure."

He obviously held office before Camp David existed.

President Polk created the Department of the Interior.

ZACHARY TAYLOR

ZACHARY TAYLOR, OUR TWELFTH president, served from 1801 to 1809.

His body was actually exhumed in 1991 due to concerns about the suspicious nature of his death. One theory suggested he had been poisoned. Experts now feel he was a victim of the unsanitary conditions of his times, and that when he fell ill, the primitive medical treatments available (including bleeding him) contributed to his death.

Mr. Taylor never voted in a presidential election.

In many ways, that makes him "a man of the people."

He had a pet horse, "Old Whitey," that visitors to the White House would pluck for horsehairs as souvenirs. (He was yet another pre-PETA president.)

Is there a situation comedy in here somewhere?

MILLARD FILLMORE

MILLARD FILLMORE, OUR THIRTEENTH president, served from 1850 to 1853.

Do you own a Toyota? Thank him. He established trade with the Japanese.

Fillmore is notable for installing the first bathtub in the White House. He was also responsible for the first stove in the White House. Prior to Fillmore, food was cooked over an open fire.

He was the first president to have a stepmother. It is not known if she was an evil one.

FRANKLIN PIERCE

OUR FOURTEENTH PRESIDENT SERVED from 1853 to 1857. His story is a sad and depressing one.

President Pierce was an alcoholic who died from cirrhosis of the liver. Before he became president, he had three children who died, one of who was decapitated in a train accident. First Lady Jane Pierce disliked the political spotlight so much that she was known as "the shadow of the White House." President Pierce sided with the Confederacy during the Civil War.

On a positive note, he oversaw the installation of central heating in the White House and was the first president to use a Christmas tree in the executive mansion.

When sworn in, he was the only president ever to say "I promise" instead of the traditional "I swear."

His tragic tenure certainly was more depressing that of Richard Nixon.

JAMES BUCHANAN

TALK ABOUT CONTROVERSY! NUMBER fifteen, who served from 1857 to 1861, is generally considered to be one of our worst presidents because he did not even try to deal with the issue of succession and the troubles between the northern and southern states. If serving today, one suspects he would certainly deny climate change.

He never married, and his niece served as official White House hostess.

Rumors about his sexuality were common, fueled by the fact that he lived with a male friend for fifteen years. Buchanan's political opponents called his friend William King "Aunt Fancy" and "Miss Nancy."

Can you imagine President Buchanan serving in a time of cable television, tabloids, and talk radio?

Certainly anyone serving before Lincoln would suffer in comparison, but Buchanan's ineptitude seemed to make Lincoln a necessity.

ABRAHAM LINCOLN

HIS FACE ADORNS THE five-dollar bill, the penny, and every license plate in Illinois. And for good reason—he emancipated the slaves, saved the Union, and made some good logs for kids to play with (okay, that last part is not true).

Number sixteen was the first president to be assassinated. He was a lawyer who never attended college. A rail-splitter. A great orator.

What I really find interesting about Abe are these things:

When he was a lawyer, he had an envelope on his desk that read: "When you can't find it anywhere else, look into this." (If he had attended law school, I would say he must have gone to school where my lawyer went to school.)

Once when he was challenged to a duel, because he was quite tall, he chose broadswords as the weapon to be used. The other guy backed down.

After his son passed away, he attended numerous séances to try to communicate with him.

All this and the Gettysburg Address.

As the great American Yakoff Smirnov would say, "What a country!"

ANDREW JOHNSON

NUMBER SEVENTEEN HAD A difficult task: following Lincoln. It was especially difficult because he ascended to the presidency due to Lincoln's assassination. Also, Johnson was a southerner, and America's Civil War had just ended.

We all know that Johnson was impeached and that he fell one vote shy of being removed from office by the United States Senate.

What many of us do not know is that he had something in common with Gandhi. Like the Mahatma, he made his own clothes. He did so his entire life.

He never attended school, so his wife taught him how to read and write.

ULYSSES S. GRANT

WAS THERE EVER A chief executive with a more presidential name? I think not.

If it were not for President Grant, we would not have the term *lobbying*. Grant used to hang out at the Willard Hotel in Washington, DC. When he would sit in the lobby, people would approach him for favors, hence the term *lobbying*.

In 1862 he issued an order requiring the removal of Jews from three different states.

President Grant received a speeding ticket while in office, resulting in the confiscation of his horse and buggy. (He had to walk home to the White House.)

On the positive side, he was instrumental in creating Yellowstone National Park.

RUTHERFORD B. HAYES

OUR NINETEENTH PRESIDENT SERVED from 1877 to 1881. He was the first president to use a telephone (his phone number was 1).

His wife started the tradition of the Easter Egg Roll on the White House grounds, a tradition that remains until this day. His first lady was called "Lemonade Lucy" because she would not serve alcoholic beverages at the White House.

The president had several pets, among which were a dog named Piccolomini and a cat named Miss Pussy.

Hayes was a Harvard Law graduate.

JAMES GARFIELD

President Garfield, our twentieth president, served only seven months.

He was our second president to be assassinated and our first left-handed president.

Many presidents claimed to be born in a log cabin, but President Garfield actually was.

Famously, he could write in Greek in one hand while simultaneously writing in Latin with his other hand.

Reportedly, President George W. Bush could write in English with his right hand.

CHESTER A. ARTHUR

OUR TWENTY-FIRST PRESIDENT SERVED from 1881 to 1885. He had something in common with President Obama: his opponents spread rumors that he was not born in the USA and was thus not eligible to serve as our president. Various rumors had him being born in Canada or Ireland. Either rumor should not have been believed, as he was not a hockey fan, nor was he a fan of Notre Dame.

President Arthur refused to move into the White House until some furniture he did not like was sold and expensive new furniture he did like was moved in.

GROVER CLEVELAND

In America, truly anyone can become president. Where else could Grover follow Chester?

Grover married a twenty-one-year-old woman while in the White House. He had been her legal guardian since she was eleven. Prior to becoming president, he had a child out of wedlock.

Grover is lucky that the *National Enquirer* and cable television were not in existence when he served.

He once proudly stated that "a sensible and responsible woman would not want to vote."

He is the only president to have served two nonconsecutive terms.

If running today, he would probably not receive an endorsement from NOW.

BENJAMIN HARRISON

PRESIDENT HARRISON, OUR TWENTY-THIRD chief executive, served from 1889 to 1893. He lost the popular vote but became president because he won the electoral vote.

Harrison had electric lights installed in the White House. He slept with the lights on, afraid he might be electrocuted if he turned them off.

Harrison was the grandson of US President William Henry Harrison.

After his wife died, he married her niece, who was twenty-five years younger than his wife.

GROVER CLEVELAND
AGAIN

GROVER WAS NOT ONLY our twenty-second president, but our twenty-fourth as well. He was our only president to serve two non-consecutive terms.

Cleveland was the first president to be filmed. He was filmed signing a bill into law.

He dedicated the Statue of Liberty and was our only president to have his wedding ceremony in the White House.

WILLIAM MCKINLEY

Mr. McKinley served from 1897 to 1901. He was our twenty-fifth president.

McKinley was the first to campaign by telephone and was the first president to ride in an automobile.

You had to admire McKinley as a family man. His wife was infirm, so instead of traveling about campaigning, he had voters transported to his home, where he would give speeches from his porch. Now here's a guy who actually practiced family values.

President McKinley was assassinated. After being shot, he requested that great care be taken in how his wife was to be told of the shooting, and he asked for assurances that the shooter not be harmed.

THEODORE ROOSEVELT

OUR TWENTY-SIXTH PRESIDENT WAS our youngest. He was forty-two when elected. On a hunting trip, he refused to shoot a captured bear, deeming it "unsportsmanlike." This was the genesis of the term *teddy bear.*

After serving, he ran for the presidency again, as a third-party candidate. Technically, he ran with the Progressive Party, but most referred to it as the "Bull Moose Party" after TR said he was "fit as a bull moose" when he was asked if he was fit to serve again.

Roosevelt won the Congressional Medal of Honor for his Spanish-American War service, most notably at the famous Battle of San Juan Hill. What makes this award remarkable is that it was won posthumously and was awarded to him by President Clinton in 2001. His great-grandson accepted on his behalf.

WILLIAM HOWARD TAFT

NUMBER TWENTY-SEVEN HELD OFFICE from 1909 to 1913. This man was big. Today he might be mistaken for an NFL lineman. Taft was so big in fact that he actually found himself stuck in the White House bathtub and needed help getting pried loose. A new bathtub was installed that could fit about four normal-sized men. William Howard was the William "Refrigerator" Perry of presidents.

Taft was the first president to throw out the first pitch at a baseball game, a tradition most presidents have followed ever since.

Taft's long-term ambition was to be a Supreme Court Justice, which he finally achieved after his presidency. He died Chief Justice of the United States.

WOODROW WILSON

OUR TWENTY-EIGHTH PRESIDENT ARGUABLY was responsible for our first female president. While in office, he suffered a significant stroke. All communication between President Wilson and the outside world was handled through his wife for a period of time while he was recovering. Many historians suspect it was Mrs. Wilson in reality making all the decisions, thus making her our de facto first female chief executive.

President Wilson won reelection in large part because of the slogan "he kept us out of war."

After winning reelection, he promptly requested a declaration of war against Germany.

WARREN G. HARDING

When Harding was a young man, he suffered a nervous breakdown. He recuperated at a sanitarium run by the Kellogg brothers, best known for inventing Corn Flakes.

Most remember President Harding as the president who served during the famous Teapot Dome scandal. This scandal will be discussed later in this book.

CALVIN COOLIDGE

OUR THIRTIETH PRESIDENT WAS an anomaly. Unlike our contemporary presidents, he believed a president should be a man of few words. It was his feeling that presidential statements would have more weight if there were fewer of them. His nickname, as a result, was "Silent Cal." If he were running today, the author would vote for him on this basis alone. A reporter once told President Coolidge that he had made a bet that he could get the president to utter more than two words that evening. President Coolidge responded, "You lose." Those were the last words he spoke that night.

An interesting fact: his father, a justice of the peace, gave him the oath of office after the death of President Harding.

HERBERT HOOVER

Many blamed President Hoover for the Great Depression. He was so reviled that the name of the Hoover Dam was changed to Boulder Dam. For a while, he was toxic and no Republican wanted anything to do with him. He was, however, a very competent man who served his nation exceedingly well as an ex-president.

When he was an ex-president, Hoover was enlisted to save Europe from starvation after World War II. His competency and hard work did just that. In fact, the name Hoover to this day means kindness in some of the Baltic countries. Hoover was able to shift world food resources to an utterly destroyed Europe, saving millions of lives in the process. Hoover lived longer than any ex-president before him and certainly rehabilitated his image by his post-presidency works. President Truman, a Democrat, used Hoover's talents quite a bit, though they were about as far apart politically as they could be. Hoover was very grateful to Truman for allowing him to serve the country as a former president.

Prior to becoming president, he became well known for his relief efforts after World War I, particularly for his economic and humanitarian work in Belgium.

Hoover holds the distinction of being the first president born west of the Mississippi. He also holds the record for catching the largest bonefish off the coast of Florida.

In his earlier days he was an eyewitness to the Boxer Rebellion, as he was living in China at the time.

To stay in shape, he invented the game "Hoover ball," a form of volleyball that utilized a medicine ball.

Herbert Hoover has two asteroids named after him: Hooveria and Hoveratta. He has no relation to the vacuums.

FRANKLIN D. ROOSEVELT

FAMOUSLY, HE BRAVELY SERVED with polio (though much of the public did not know this), guided us through the Depression and World War II, and was our only president elected four times. Many historians consider him one of our greatest presidents, this author included. There is a great deal of interesting trivia about FDR (our first president referred to commonly by his initials).

Teddy Roosevelt, a former president himself and a fourth cousin of FDR, gave Roosevelt's wife away at her wedding. Teddy said he wanted to "keep the name in the family." Teddy was Eleanor's uncle.

How he found the time we do not know, but Franklin Roosevelt was an avid stamp collector, having one of the biggest stamp collections in existence.

Like Teddy Roosevelt, Franklin too served as Secretary of the Navy at one time.

The term *New Deal*, the name for Roosevelt's economic plan to help the nation recover from the Depression, was suggested by Mark Twain, FDR's favorite writer, who used the term in the novel *A Connecticut Yankee in King Arthur's Court*.

Before becoming president, while recovering from polio, FDR wrote a screenplay but was not able to get Hollywood to make the movie.

Roosevelt was the first American president to have the British royal family sleep over at the White House. He served them hot dogs. Remarkably, this did not set back Anglo-American relations.

HARRY S. TRUMAN

HARRY TRUMAN IS CERTAINLY one of our more colorful presidents. He was relatively unknown on the national level before becoming FDR's vice president, though he was never close to FDR. In fact, he did not know about the atomic bomb until FDR died and Truman became president.

Truman integrated the armed forces, which was considered a bold and risky political move at the time. He also fired General Douglas McArthur during the Korean War for not obeying orders, another bold move given McArthur was much more popular than the president.

Truman was outspoken and rather colorful in his language, prompting his supporters to urge, "Give 'em hell, Harry!" Truman always said he did not give them hell; he gave them the truth, which was hell to them.

When Truman's daughter, who eventually became a well-known mystery writer, received a bad review from a columnist for a dance recital, Truman sent him a nasty letter and threatened to punch him in the nose (what father wouldn't?).

Truman's mother was the daughter of a prominent Confederate officer. As such she was imprisoned for a short time in an internment camp. When Truman was president, she refused to stay in the Lincoln bedroom when visiting her son in the White House, due to her lingering resentment of the Union. Late in life, she was mad at

Harry for giving a speech and being photographed at the Lincoln Memorial.

When in Mexico City, against the advice of his aides, he insisted on laying a wreath at the gravesite of Mexican soldiers who died during the Mexican-American War. This endeared him to the Mexican people and made him unpopular with a whole lot of Texans.

Known for having the sign "The buck stops here" on his desk as president, he had an even better sign on his desk when serving in the US Senate: "Always do right. This will gratify some people and astonish the rest."

When campaigning for JFK, he was quoted as saying Nixon never told the truth a day in his life. A wise man, that Harry S. Truman.

The *S* in Harry S. Truman did not stand for anything. Harry did, though, and is considered one of America's greatest presidents.

Truman was the first person to receive a social security check. His social security number was 1.

DWIGHT D. EISENHOWER

AFTER COMMANDING OUR TROOPS during World War II, Eisenhower became the President of Columbia University, an Ivy League school in New York City. The former general walked across Central Park to work and carried a gun to protect himself.

Eisenhower was so popular after commanding our armies during World War II that both political parties wanted him to run for president. President Harry Truman lobbied Eisenhower to run as a Democrat. Truman even offered to not run himself and support Ike if Eisenhower ran as a Democrat. Of course, Ike eventually decided to run, and won two terms, as a Republican.

Eisenhower was lukewarm in endorsing his vice president, Richard Nixon, when Nixon ran against Kennedy in 1960 for the presidency. When asked if Nixon accomplished anything while in office, Ike replied that if he was given a week, he might think of something that Nixon accomplished.

In his post-presidency days, Ike gave frequent advice to President Kennedy about the Cuban Missile Crisis and to President Johnson about the Vietnam War. He was, after all, one of America's greatest generals.

JOHN F. KENNEDY

OUR THIRTY-FIFTH PRESIDENT HAS had so much written about him that there are few little-known facts.

Kennedy, and the Kennedy name, was so popular in Massachusetts that an unrelated (and unqualified) man also named John F. Kennedy was elected as treasurer of Massachusetts in 1958.

As we all know, the Kennedy family was, and is, extremely wealthy. JFK almost never carried money and relied on his aides and employees to use theirs to pay for anything that was necessary when Kennedy was out and about. He rarely made an effort to pay them back.

Kennedy was so popular that his approval ratings actually soared after a botched invasion of Cuba. Kennedy was amazed that this could happen. Can you imagine how Jimmy Carter must have felt when his popularity plummeted after a failed rescue attempt of American hostages in Iran?

LYNDON B. JOHNSON

NUMBER THIRTY-SIX IS RESPECTED for pushing for civil rights, knowing full well that doing so would cost his party votes for generations to come. LBJ was known for his ribald humor and competency as a legislative leader.

Lost in most accounts of LBJ is that he was a decorated soldier.

Though he escalated the Vietnam War, doing so tore him apart internally. He once went with his daughter at midnight to a DC-area church to pray that he had not started World War III after he ordered the mining of harbors in North Vietnam.

RICHARD NIXON

NIXON WAS OUR ONLY president to resign. He resigned in disgrace to avoid a certain impeachment. By most accounts, he was able to substantially rehabilitate his image after his presidency.

After leaving office, Nixon was a prolific and well-respected author of books about foreign affairs. Nixon's knowledge of foreign affairs, especially on all matters Russian, led to President Bill Clinton frequently seeking his advice.

In his early days as a politician, Nixon was well known as an anti-Communist. This is what allowed him to seek out normal relations with Communist China without being viewed as being weak. Indeed, an important political phrase resulted from this effort that is very true: "Only Nixon could go to China."

In a Star Trek movie, it was necessary for The Federation (of which Earth was a part) to make peace with the evil Klingon Empire. To do so, they had to rely on the most well-known Klingon hater, Captain James T. Kirk. When asked why Kirk was chosen to make the peace, his sidekick, the Vulcan Mr. Spock, stated, "We have a saying on Vulcan: only Nixon can go to China."

GERALD FORD

PRESIDENT FORD, AS WE know, was not elected vice president nor elected president. He is either admired or reviled for pardoning his predecessor, Richard Nixon. Admired for trying to heal the nation by pardoning Nixon and having the "national nightmare" end, or reviled for pardoning the president who disgraced the nation.

Our thirty-eighth president was often mocked by comics for being a klutz, due to his frequent trips and falls. He was anything but a klutz, having played college football well enough to be offered contracts by two professional football teams. Ford also coached the Yale boxing team when he was a young man. He was hardly a klutz.

Gerald Ford was our first president to have been an Eagle Scout, as well as our first president whose parents were divorced.

When Ford was a young man, he worked as a fashion model, a job his eventual wife, Betty, also had.

Ford was born Leslie Lynch King Jr. and was adopted by his stepfather and renamed Jerry Ford after him. Ford did not find out he was adopted until he was twelve.

Ford was the last living member of the Warren Commission, which was charged with investigating the assassination of President Kennedy. So it is possible that any secrets about the Kennedy assassination may have died with Ford.

Being a congressman, vice president, and president, as well as being a soldier, were not Ford's only government jobs. He was once a park ranger at Yellowstone National Park.

President Ford was right-handed but wrote left-handed.

President Ford became a very wealthy man after his presidency by giving speeches and sitting on corporate boards. He became a prominent citizen of Palm Springs as well as Vale, Colorado, in his retirement.

JIMMY CARTER

IF EVER THERE WAS a long shot for the presidency, it was Jimmy Carter. A one-term Georgia governor, he came out of nowhere to win the presidency. Being viewed as an honest man probably helped after the nation had endured Richard Nixon and Ford's courageous (?) pardon.

Jimmy Carter was a peanut farmer from a small Georgia town before becoming governor of that state. He also served as a nuclear submarine commander.

While he was president, and even today, he regularly taught Sunday school classes at his home church in Plains, Georgia.

In many ways, Carter was viewed as an ineffectual president but has been much admired for his work in his post-presidency years.

RONALD REAGAN

WHEN OUR FORTIETH PRESIDENT worked as an actor, he was a union president and wrote eloquently on behalf of union causes. When president, he fired members of the Air Traffic Controllers union and was less than union friendly.

During World War II, Reagan served in the motion picture unit of the army, starring in training films and propaganda pieces.

As a young man, Reagan was a radio broadcaster doing play-by-play announcing for Chicago Cub games. He was not physically at the games but made up the action based on a ticker tape account of the game. No one was the wiser.

Two of his sons went on to become prominent radio broadcasters themselves. His son Ron Jr. became a liberal radio talk show host, and his son Michael a conservative (like his father) talk show host. Reagan's daughter posed for *Playboy* magazine. (Twice actually—once at fifty-eight years of age.)

GEORGE H. W. BUSH

OUR FORTY-FIRST PRESIDENT WAS a legitimate war hero. He was our youngest bomber pilot during World War II. Much to his credit, like another famous American politician, George McGovern, he never tried to capitalize on this in any of his campaigns for office.

After the Kennedy assassination, Mr. Bush actually contacted the government with some theories on who he thought might have been behind the killing.

Many people forget that Bush served not only as CIA Director but also as Ambassador to China. Who said only Nixon could go to China?

WILLIAM J. CLINTON

BILL CLINTON, LIKE JERRY Ford before him, took the last name of his stepfather. Clinton was the first president who was a Rhodes scholar.

Bill Clinton seriously considered becoming a professional musician when he was younger.

To pay off the massive legal bills he ran up due to the Lewinsky scandal, he earned a great deal of money on the speaking circuit after his presidency.

GEORGE W. BUSH

"W" MADE HISTORY BY appointing the first African American woman, Condoleezza Rice, to a prominent government position as secretary of state.

Before September 11, 2011, Bush planned on making educational reform his signature accomplishment. Of course 9/11 changed all that.

Bush did not make a single veto in his first term.

When he won the nomination, he wanted input as to whom he should pick as vice president. He appointed a family confidant to head this search committee and recommend a running mate. The head of the search committee: Dick Cheney.

BARACK OBAMA

OUR FORTY-FOURTH PRESIDENT WILL always be remembered as the Jackie Robinson of the oval office: our first African American president.

Obama is distantly related to former Vice President Dick Cheney.

Obama's father, who was from Kenya, left a wife in Kenya and married Obama's mother when they were both college students in Hawaii.

President Obama was raised for the most part by his grandparents in Hawaii. His mother (whose first name was Stanley) became a well-respected anthropologist.

Obama is the first president to be a die-hard Chicago White Sox fan. He often expresses admiration for former Republican President Ronald Reagan, who used to work as a broadcaster of Chicago Cubs games. As a Chicagoan, I find this very unlikely, but it's true nonetheless.

PART THREE

PRESIDENTIAL SCANDALS

TWO FORGOTTEN SCANDALS

WATERGATE, LEWINSKY, TEAPOT DOME, the Plame Affair: we have had some blockbuster scandals. But there are two that are often forgotten.

THE WHISKEY RING

Grant's administration was noted for its many scandals. The most significant one was the Whiskey Ring. Many government officials benefited from tax revenues obtained from whiskey distillers and alcohol distributers. It is thought that Grant was not personally involved, but his private secretary was. Three million dollars of inappropriate taxation was discovered, and eventually 110 people were convicted. A scandal this large would be difficult for a president to weather today.

TRUMAN'S FREEZER

Many important members of Truman's administration were investigated for receiving gifts (including freezers and fur coats) for various favors granted. The IRS investigated the situation, which led to the resignation of over 150 government employees. The attorney general fired a special prosecutor that was doing his job too well. Truman then sacked the attorney general. Truman's own wife received a deep freezer from a businessman who had been given a favor by a Truman aide.

PART FOUR

THE REALLY ODD FACTS

1. Jimmy Carter was the first president born in a hospital.
2. Calvin Coolidge often had his head rubbed with Vaseline while he was having breakfast in bed. He also used to ring the White House doorbell and hide.
3. Warren G. Harding lost the White House china in a poker game.
4. Taft could have eaten Madison for breakfast. Taft weighed three hundred pounds, Madison under one hundred.
5. Thomas Jefferson has many descendents from his liaisons with his slave Sally Hemmings.

PART FIVE

THE VICE PRESIDENTS

CHESTER A. ARTHUR SERVED as Garfield's vice president and eventually as president himself. Early in his career he was the collector for the Port of New York and received a great deal of money in kickbacks. Rumors abounded that he was born in Canada, which would have disqualified him from being vice president. Nonetheless, he was.

HENRY WALLACE, FDR's SECOND VP, secretly sent government officials to Asia to investigate a possible visit there from Christ. Wallace became a big supporter of the Soviet Union. Dumped by FDR, he later ran for president as a progressive. He finished his life doing agricultural research on his farm.

WILLIAM RUFUS DE VANE King was sworn in as vice president while in Cuba, where he was recovering from tuberculosis and alcoholism.

ANDREW JOHNSON, LINCOLN'S VICE president, was severely drunk when he was sworn in as president following Lincoln's assassination.

AARON BURR, THOMAS JEFFERSON's VP, shot Alexander Hamilton in a duel. He also plotted to become emperor of the western United States and Mexico. When he was turned in for this plot, he approached Napoleon for help in becoming the leader of what is now Florida. When he was seventy-six, he married a wealthy widow and plundered her financial resources. She divorced him for his many infidelities. The divorce was granted on the very day Burr died.